Summertime with My Best Friend

Written By: Danielle White

Illustrated By: Valeria Leonova

Mullen Press

4600 Powder Mill Rd Suite 450

Beltsville, Maryland 20705

www.mullenpress.com

Ilustrator: Valeria Leonova

Ordering Information: Special discounts are available on quantity purchases by corporations, associations, and others. For details, contact the publisher at the address above.

Summertime with My Best Friend / Danielle White — First Edition

ISBN 978-1-7020701-9-5 (Hardback)

ISBN 978-1-7323458-6-7 (Paperback)

ISBN 978-1-7323458-7-4 (Ebook)

Printed in the United States of America

ACKNOWLEDGMENTS

All praises must first go to God. Completing this book challenged me to step out of my comfort zone, not staying in fear, but to live a more faith-filled life. John 10:10, "the thief comes to steal, kill, and destroy; I have come that they may have life and have it to the full." Special thanks to my two daughters, Sariah Emani and Justice Renee, for the inspiration to share our story and memories. To my family that has instilled so much love and support throughout this process, you all encouraged me to move forward in sharing my unforgettable bond with my Grandmother.

Dedicated to the loving memory of Marilyn White

"Grandmother."

Summertime with My Best Friend

Woo-Hoo! It's my favorite time of year, Summertime! Do you know what that means? I'm going to my Grandmother's house! While others are just glad to be out of school, I'm twice as glad to spend time with her.

It is a tradition of ours that started when I was a baby. She allows me to just be a kid and have fun. She's also a great person for me to look up to. She calls me her little Dani Pie, and to me, she is the best Grandmother in the world!

Rules? There are no rules at Grandmother's house. We stay up late, eat snacks, play games, and laugh ourselves to sleep. I get to play in her clothes, try on her jewelry, and don't tell my parents, but she even lets me drink soda when it starts getting late. She's not just my Grandmother; she's my best friend.

When I call my Grandmother, she can hear me smiling through the phone.

"Grandmother! Grandmother! Are you home?" I ask excitedly.

"My Dani Pie! Yes, I am, are you coming today?"

I said, "I am, I am; we're on the way."

On the way to Grandmother's house, I think about all the new things I can tell her about school and what movies we can watch. Then before too long, we're turning onto Winterberry Lane.

Getting out of the car, I hear my Grandmother's voice from the window. She was waiting for us to get here.

"Is that my Dani Pie I see?" she asks with a big smile on her face.

"Grandmother, yes, it's me!" I laugh as she drops down her house key.

Running through the door, up the stairs, I see her in the kitchen. We share the tightest hug, and she gives me the biggest kiss on my cheek.

"Grandmother, I miss you! I'm so happy to see you!"

"Oh, my Dani Pie, you're getting so big. I missed you, too."

As my Grandmother and my parents talk, I unpack my toys to get settled. She has a den full of things that we can do together. There is a big TV for movies, a chalkboard for playing school, a riding pony, and Barbies everywhere. It mostly stays the same from my last visit, but she always surprises me with a few new toys.

After kissing my parents good-bye, I look up to my Grandmother and ask, "So, what are we doing today?"

It was getting a little late, so she said, "How about you help me with dinner, and we watch a movie for the night?"

"Sounds good to me, what are we making?"

She looks at me, smiles, and together we yell, "PIZZA!"

Putting on our aprons, I grab the pepperoni and cheese from the refrigerator, and she picks out everything else. After spreading the dough, we add the toppings, and Grandmother puts it in the oven.

Then, we laugh together on the couch eating pizza and watching a movie. This is a great start for our Summertime together.

In the morning, Grandmother wakes me with the sweet smell of her famous bowl of oatmeal. Not one but three.

"Child, your stomach is going to pop! Where do you put all of this food?" she giggles.

"I don't know, Grandmother, it's just so good, I can't stop."

In the afternoon, as she watches TV, I decide to put on a fashion show. I go to her closet, pull down clothes, and model outfits one by one.

She narrates and describes my outfits as I walk confidently across the floor in her heels.

"Here," she said, "We have Danielle covered in the finest of cotton t-shirts, leopard pants, red heels, and black church hat. Isn't she lovely?" said Grandmother as I return to the closet and take a bow.

Now that the fashion show is over, we move on to do something else.

"How about we color, you can tell me about school, and your new friends," said Grandmother.

"Ok," I said as I hurried to find the perfect books. While coloring, I also tell her about a new dance I learned.

She asks me to show her some moves and even tries to do them herself. Watching her dance is so funny because she never gets it right, but I sure do love to see her try.

Besides going to school to make new friends, she also encourages me to do well in class and to be a good example. She's really good at math, which is my least favorite, but with her help, I'm learning to like it more.

Shortly after, we hear a knock at the door and it's my friends. I don't see them often during the school year, so in the Summer, we get to play outside all day. There's a playground across the street from my Grandmother's house. Sometimes she didn't come outside with me, but I could always look to the kitchen window and see her standing there.

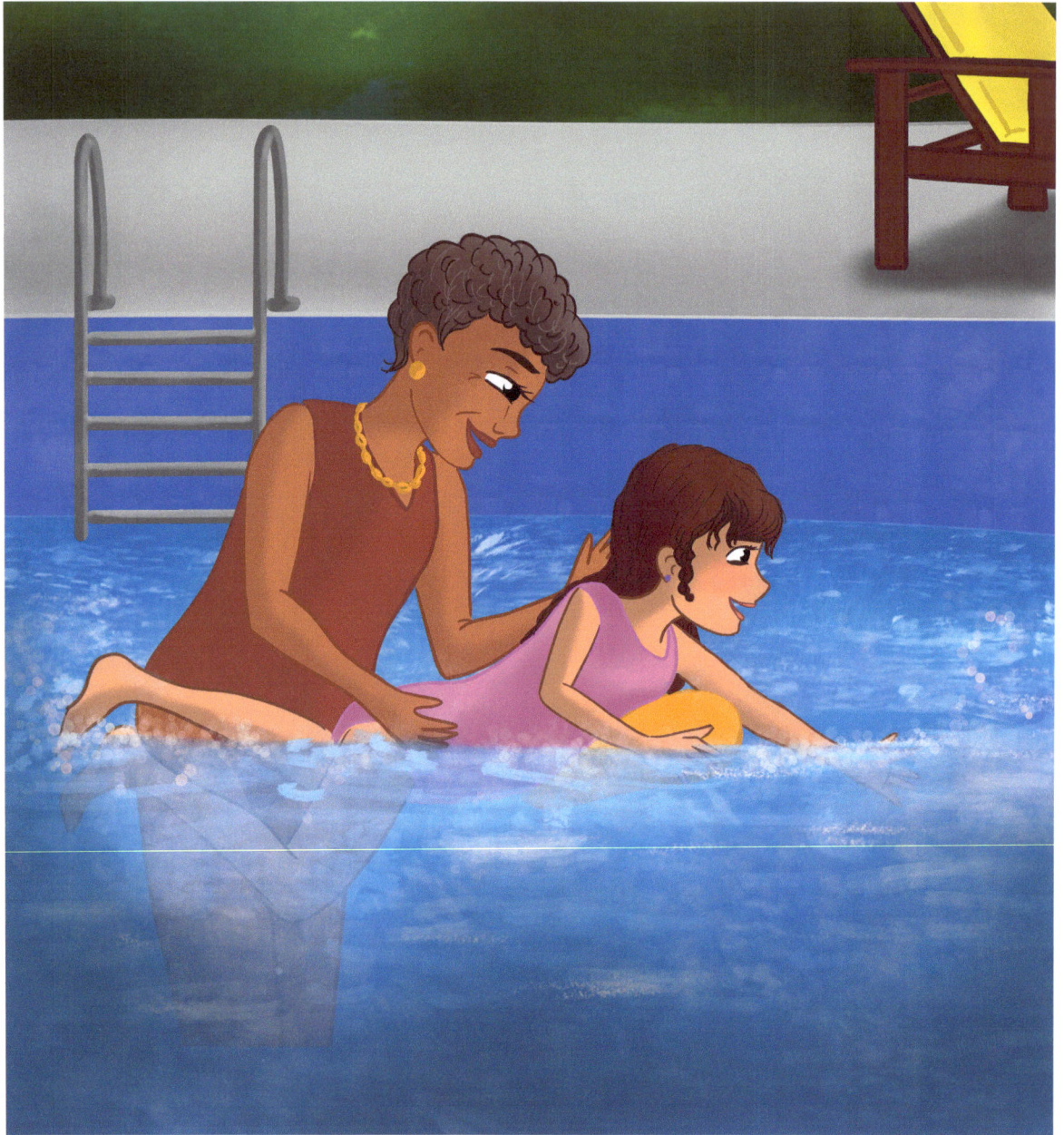

Once the street lights started to come on, I knew it was time to go in the house. My Grandmother would prepare a hot bath with many bubbles and toys to keep me company. She sings my favorite lullaby and rubs my head until I fall asleep.

Throughout the weeks, she allows me to choose between going to the beach and going to the pool. We both were like little fish that stayed in the water until our fingers and toes looked like prunes.

She taught me how to swim on my back which was scary. However, I always wanted to learn after seeing her do it many times before.

Showing her all of my tricks for jumping in the pool, she would always be so excited to see them as if it were her first time.

"Look at me Grandmother! Watch this!"

"Yay! That's my Dani Pie!"

Back and forth, I would jump tirelessly.

Four weeks of summer were going by so quickly, and it was almost time for me to go back home. The night before I would leave, we make my favorite pineapple pound cake. In the morning, we ate a slice with a cold glass of milk for breakfast. It was absolutely delicious.

When my parents got here to pick me up, I was happy to see them but sad that it was time for me to go. We had another great summer full of good memories that will last forever.

Not many people get the chance to have a best friend. I'm lucky to have my Grandmother, my best friend.

The End

Author Bio

Danielle White published her first book, "Summertime with My Best Friend," in 2020. It is a memorial to her late grandmother, Marilyn White. She is also the founder of Style N G.R.A.C.E, an event planning and management company in the Washington, D.C. metropolitan area. Learn more about Danielle White and her upcoming works at DanielleRWhite.com.

www.ingramcontent.com/pod-product-compliance
Lightning Source LLC
LaVergne TN
LVHW072100070426
835508LV00002B/199